a gift for

my love ♥

from

Krisel

08.19.07

LOVERS

a giftbook

M·I·L·K

MOMENTS INTIMACY LAUGHTER KINSHIP

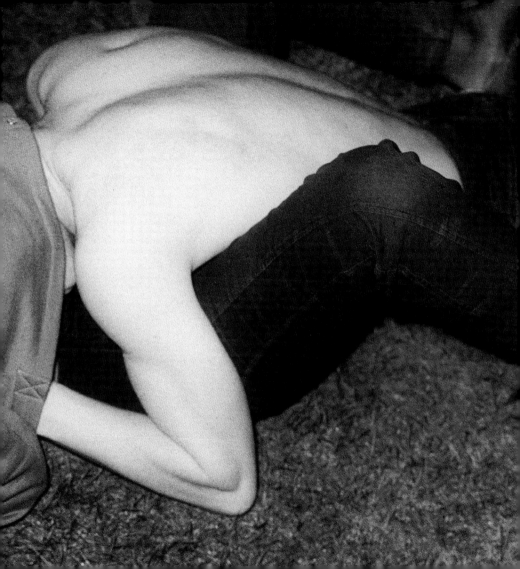

Let's do it,
let's fall in love.

[COLE PORTER]

How do I **love** thee?

Let me count the ways.

[ELIZABETH BARRETT BROWNING]

Two people who
belong together
make a world.

[HANS MARGOLIUS]

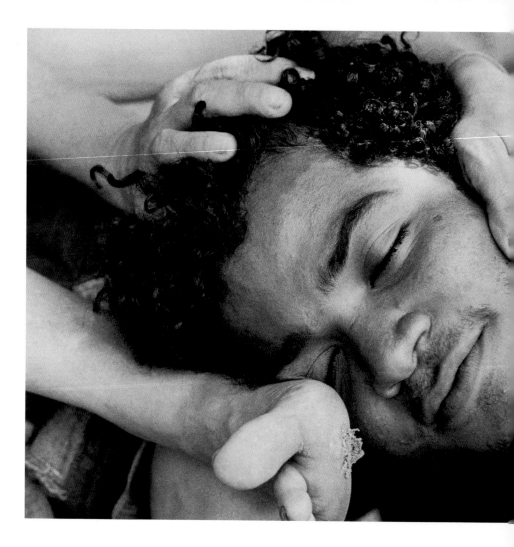

I live for those who love me,
for those who **know** me true.

[GEORGE LINNAEUS BANKS]

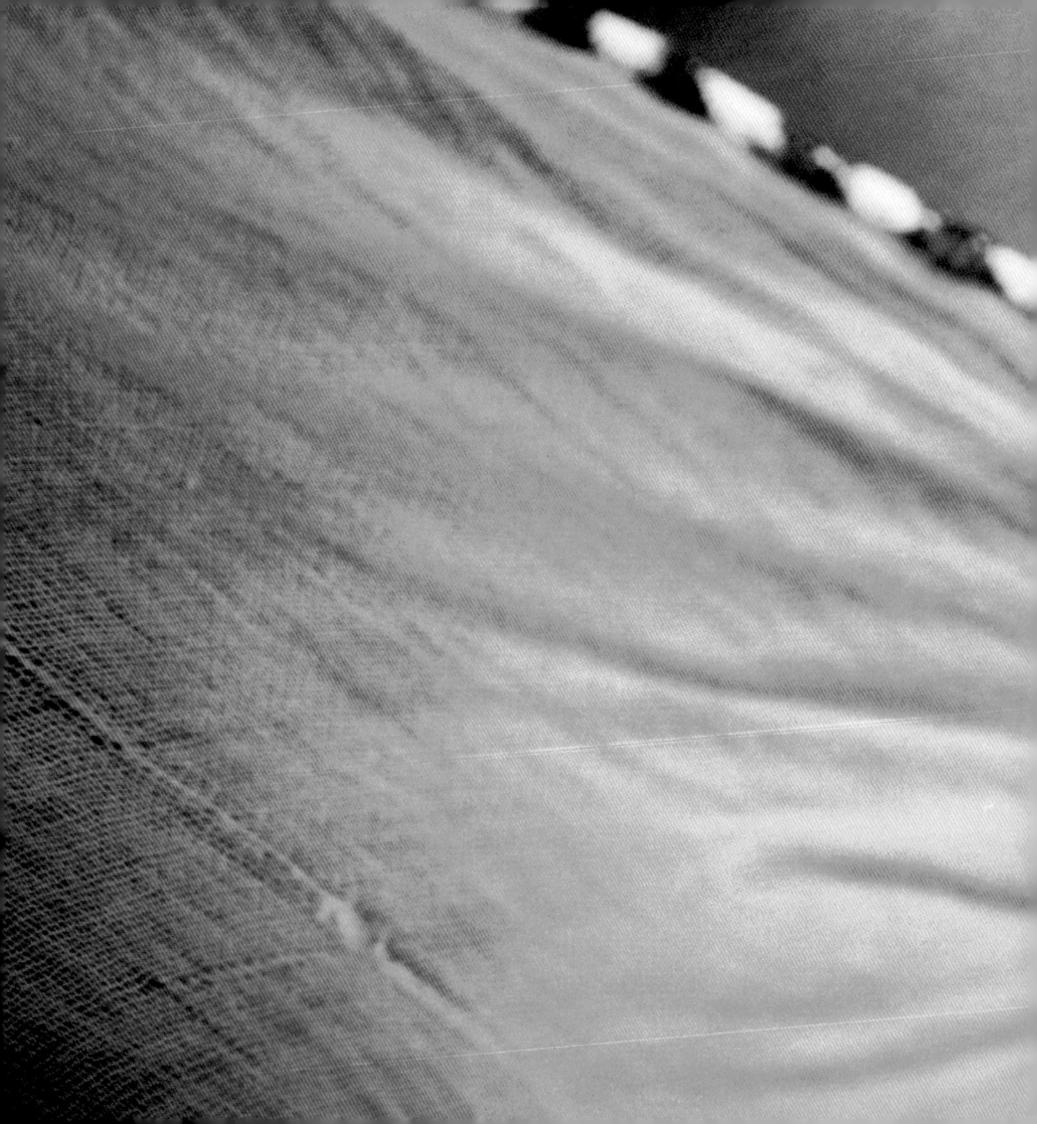

Love does not consist in gazing at each other

but looking outward together in the same direction.

[ANTOINE SAINT-EXUPERY]

You will find as you look
back upon your life that the moments
when you have truly lived are the moments
when you have done things in the
spirit of love

[HENRY DRUMMOND]

Page 2
© Everett Kennedy Brown, Japan

On a journey through the steppes of Inner Mongolia in China, new friends pause to feed their horses and to share a moment of quiet affection.

Pages 4–5
© Gundula Schulze-Eldowy, Germany

Photographer Gundula Schulze-Eldowy can't help laughing as her friend Stephen tickles her. She set the camera on automatic to capture this spontaneous self-portrait in a local park near her home in the Pankow district of Berlin, Germany.

Pages 6–7
© Jindřich Štreit, Czech Republic

Boy meets girl – in the small village of Kižinga in Southern Siberia, Russia.

Pages 8-9
© Tzer Luck Lau, Singapore

Intimacy does not require privacy when you're a teenager living in Manhattan. These young students are absorbed in their own passionate world on a busy street in New York, USA.

Page 10
© Romano Cagnoni, Italy

On a beach in Cleethorpes, England, a fairground rocket provides the backdrop for a young couple's playful romp in the sand.

Page 11
© Richard Frank, USA

Putting your feet up takes on a new meaning in Indiana, USA.

Pages 12–13
© David Sanchez Gimenez, Spain

A cheeky young couple distracts Alfonso from his newspaper as he waits for his bus in Barcelona, Spain.

Page 15
© Marcio RM, Brazil

As the parade passes by in the Rio de Janeiro carnival, Brazil, a young couple share an affectionate kiss amid the crowd.

Pages 16–17
© Tommy Agriodimas, USA

A young girl gazes at an attractive passer-by on a sunlit street in Apithia, Greece.

Page 18
© Tino Soriano, Spain

Rain delays the beginning of a carnival in Barahona, Dominican Republic. A young couple exchange a flirtatious glance as they wait for the festivities to begin.

Page 19
© Vincent Delbrouck, Belgium

Young lovers clasp each other tight as they dance to the rhythms of Havana, Cuba.

Page 20
© Todd Davis, USA

Bob drives his wife, Peggy, home to Houston, Texas, USA. The couple have been married for 54 years.

Page 21
© Sam Devine Tischler, USA

The photographer captured this affectionate image of his grandfather Max, 86, and grandmother Ann, 80, in New Port Richie, Florida, USA.

Pages 22–23
© Christophe Agou, USA

On a crowded subway train in New York, USA, a young couple only have eyes for each other.

Page 25
© Sandra Eleta, Panama

The spirit of the old Latin American phrase "tienes luz en la pupila" – "you have light in your eyes" – is captured in this photograph of Putulungo and Alma, taken in Portobelo, Panama.

Pages 26–27
© Ricardo Serpa, Brazil

While the traffic rumbles by on the streets of Rio de Janeiro, Brazil, a homeless man sleeps serenely with some support from a friend.

Pages 28–29 and front cover
© Ivan Coleman, UK

London, England – two tourists share a lingering kiss by the water as the sun sets on a busy day of sightseeing.

Page 30
© Renate Pfleiderer, USA

Newly wedded bliss on Long Island, New York – Travis catches Camille's wedding veil when it blows off in the wind, but he can't resist trying it on before returning it to his new wife.

Page 31
© Melissa Mermin, USA
Wedding preparations in Boston, USA against all tradition, the groom, Doug, sneaks a kiss from his bride, Jennifer, before they get dressed for the occasion.

Pages 32–33
© Katherine Fletcher, USA
At a wedding in Omaha, Nebraska, USA, a young guest hides her eyes as a newly married couple share a kiss; her young friend is unperturbed.

Pages 34–35
© Dmitri Korobeinikov, Russia
In the Russian village of Gimenej, heavy rain turns the road to mud on a couple's wedding day. The bridegroom helps to push the car as his bride seeks sanctuary from the weather.

Pages 36–37
© Alan Berner, USA
English Bay beach in Vancouver, Canada – a newly wed couple are in a playful mood as they wait for their wedding portrait to be taken.

Page 39
© Vladimir Kryukov, Russia
After a swim in the chilly waters of a Moscow river, a Russian couple steal the show with a display of affection.

Pages 40–41
© Bill Frakes, USA
In tandem – a novel way of moving house captured on film in Miami Beach, Florida, USA.

Pages 42–43
© Mikhail Evstafiev, Russia
On the streets of Santiago de Cuba, Cuba a couple's uninhibited display of affection raises a spontaneous smile from their young audience.

Pages 44–45
© Jamshid Bayrami, Iran
Chahbahar in the Persian Gulf Littoral – Sahel waits anxiously for her fisherman boyfriend to return from sea. When asked about her lover's whereabouts, she covers her face to hide her tears.

Page 47
© Romualdas Požerskis, Lithuania
In a small town in Lithuania, families come together once a year for their own Catholic pilgrimage. After a day of celebration, two elderly relatives bid each other farewell before heading home.

Pages 48–49
© José Caldas, Brazil
A married couple stand side by side in their home by the São Francisco River, Brazil. Behind them, their wedding picture is proudly displayed.

Pages 50–51
© Piotr Malecki, Poland
A train station in Tallinn, Estonia, is the setting for tearful farewells as sailors from the Russian fleet say goodbye to their Estonian girlfriends.

Page 52
© David Hancock, Australia
Sharing sunshine and shopping on a day trip to Manly, a seaside suburb of Sydney, Australia.

Page 53
© Robert Lifson, USA
A farmer looks up to his wife in the rural village of Ruseni, Romania.

Page 54
© Harvey Stein, USA
An amorous pair share hugs and kisses on a doorstep in Florence, Italy, oblivious to the passers-by.

Page 55
© Josef Sekal, Czech Republic
A park bench makes a change from the sofa for an elderly couple winding a ball of wool in Prague, Czech Republic.

Page 57
© Karen Maini, USA
A peaceful moment at the Zen Mountain Monastery on Mount Tremper, in the state of New York, USA.

Pages 58–59 and back cover
© Y Nagasaki, USA
Holding hands in the surf, an elderly couple get away from it all on Sandy Hook beach in New Jersey, USA.

Pages 60–61
© Ricardo Ordóñez, Canada
The 60th wedding anniversary – love, respect and six decades of marriage bind husband and wife Henri and Violet Mayoux. They exchange a humorous look as they prepare to cut their anniversary cake in Ontario, Canada.

Inspired by the 1950s landmark photographic exhibition, *"The Family of Man,"* M.I.L.K. began as an epic global search to develop a collection of extraordinary and geographically diverse images portraying humanity's Moments of Intimacy, Laughter and Kinship (M.I.L.K.). This search took the form of a photographic competition – probably the biggest, and almost certainly the most ambitious of its kind ever to be conducted. With a world-record prize pool, and renowned Magnum photographer Elliott Erwitt as Chief Judge, the M.I.L.K. competition attracted 17,000 photographers from 164 countries. Three hundred winning images were chosen from the over 40,000 photographs submitted to form the basis of the M.I.L.K. Collection.

The winning photographs were first published as three books titled *Family*, *Friendship* and *Love* in early 2001, and are now featured in a range of products worldwide, in nine languages in more than 20 countries. The M.I.L.K. Collection also forms the basis of an international travelling exhibition.

The M.I.L.K. Collection portrays unforgettable images of human life, from its first fragile moments to its last. They tell us that the rich bond that exists between families and friends is universal. Representing many diverse cultures, the compelling and powerful photographs convey feelings experienced by people around the globe. Transcending borders, the M.I.L.K. imagery reaches across continents to celebrate and reveal the heart of humanity.

www.milkphotos.com

© 2004 PQ Publishers Limited. Published under license from M.I.L.K. Licensing Limited.

All copyrights of the photographic images are owned by the individual photographers who have granted M.I.L.K. Licensing Limited the right to use them.

First published by Helen Exley Giftbooks in 2004, 16 Chalk Hill, Watford, Herts, WD19 4BG, UK.
www.helenexleygiftbooks.com

12 11 10 9 8 7 6 5 4 3 2

ISBN 1-86187-926-1

Designed by Kylie Nicholls. Printed by Midas Printing International Limited, China. Back cover quotation by Goethe.

MOMENTS INTIMACY LAUGHTER KINSHIP